First Facts®

MY FIRST GUIDE TO
PAPER AIRPLANES

by Christopher Harbo

CAPSTONE PRESS
a capstone imprint

First Facts are published by Capstone Press,
1710 Roe Crest Drive, North Mankato, Minnesota 56003
www.capstonepub.com

Library of Congress Cataloging-in-Publication Data
Harbo, Christopher L.
  My first guide to paper airplanes / by Christopher Harbo.
    pages cm.—(First facts. My first guides)
  Includes bibliographical references.
  Summary: "Step-by-step photo-illustrated instructions show how to fold a variety of simple paper airplanes"—Provided by publisher.
  Audience: K–3.
  ISBN 978-1-4914-2047-8 (library binding)
  ISBN 978-1-4914-2253-3 (eBook PDF)
1. Paper airplanes—Juvenile literature. I. Title.
  TL778.H37345 2015
  745.592—dc23   2014032620

Editorial Credits

Kathryn Clay and Alesha Sullivan, editors; Tracy McCabe, designer;
Jo Miller, media researcher; Katy LaVigne, production specialist

Photo Credits

All Photos by Capstone Studio: Karon Dubke except: Shutterstock: koya979, cover (top left), 1

Design elements

Shutterstock: Aleks Melnik, sommthink, TashaNatasha

Printed in the United States of America in North Mankato, Minnesota.
092014   008482CGS15

TABLE OF CONTENTS

Ready for Takeoff

Grab your pilot goggles and strap yourself in for takeoff! These paper airplanes are prepped and ready to send you soaring. From the classic Long-Distance Dart to the wacky Duck Plane, these folded flyers are super easy to make. In minutes, you'll turn a lazy afternoon into an amazing airborne adventure!

FOLDING SYMBOLS

Fold the paper in the direction of the arrow.

Fold the paper behind.

Fold the paper and then unfold it.

Turn the paper over or rotate it (turn it sideways).

A fold or edge hidden under another layer of paper; also used to mark where to cut with a scissors.

MATERIALS

Every paper airplane builder needs a well-stocked toolbox. The models in this book use the materials listed below:

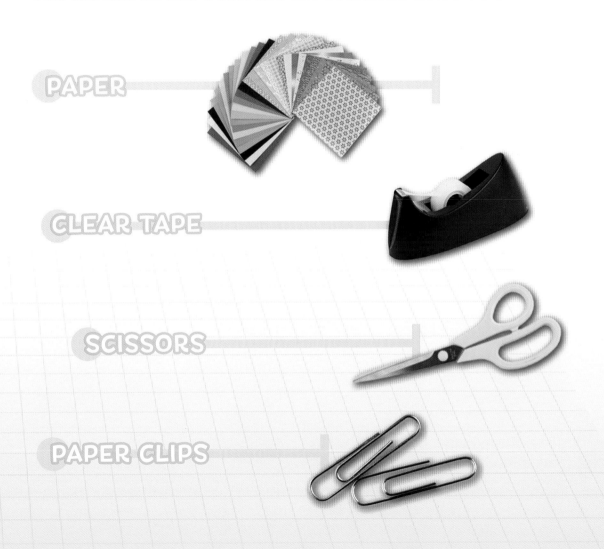

PAPER

CLEAR TAPE

SCISSORS

PAPER CLIPS

Long-Distance Dart

The Long-Distance Dart is the perfect model for contests. It zips through the air, straight and fast.

START HERE

MATERIALS

- 8.5- by 11-inch (22- by 28-centimeter) paper

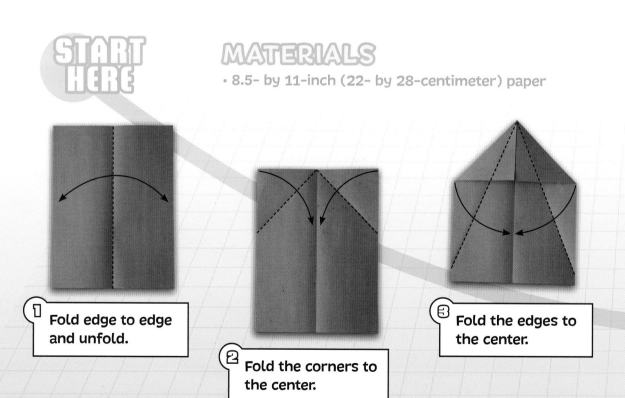

1 Fold edge to edge and unfold.

2 Fold the corners to the center.

3 Fold the edges to the center.

7 Finished Long-Distance Dart

END HERE

FLYING TIP

Use a medium throw with a slight upward angle.

6 Lift the wings.

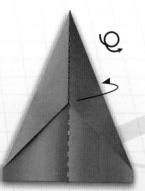

5 Fold the top layer even with the bottom edge. Repeat behind.

4 Fold the right side behind and rotate.

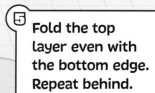

7

Flutterby

The Flutterby may be the simplest paper flier you will ever fold. With two quick creases, a strip of paper acts like a fluttering butterfly.

START HERE

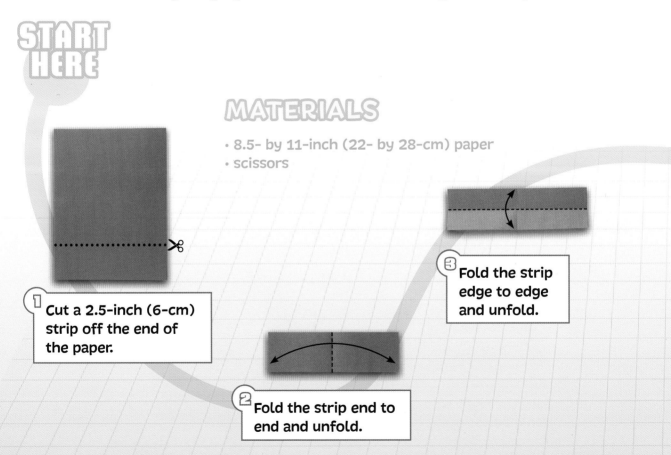

MATERIALS

- 8.5- by 11-inch (22- by 28-cm) paper
- scissors

1 Cut a 2.5-inch (6-cm) strip off the end of the paper.

2 Fold the strip end to end and unfold.

3 Fold the strip edge to edge and unfold.

④ Cut the strip on the creases made in steps 2 and 3.

⑤ Fold the ends of one small rectangle. Allow these flaps to stand up.

⑥ Finished Flutterby

END HERE

FLYING TIP

Pinch the middle of the model. Release with a gentle, forward push. The higher you hold it, the longer it will flutter.

9

Whirligig

Give the Whirligig a spin! This clever model looks like a paper helicopter as it twirls to the ground.

START HERE

MATERIALS

- 8.5- by 11-inch (22- by 28-cm) paper
- scissors
- large paper clip

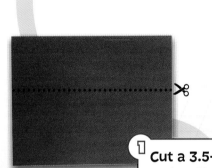

1 Cut a 3.5-inch (9-cm) strip off the paper's long side.

2 Cut a 5-inch (13-cm) slit down the center of the strip.

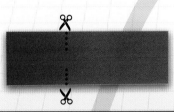

3 Cut two 1.25-inch (3-cm) slits in the sides of the strip. These slits should be about 4 inches (10 cm) from the bottom of the strip.

4 Fold the flaps.

5 Fold the bottom edge.

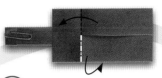

6 Attach a paper clip to the folded edge.

7 Fold one wing forward. Fold the other wing to the back.

FLYING TIP

Hold onto the paper clip. Throw the model straight up into the air as high as you can. Watch it spin to the ground.

END HERE

8 Finished Whirligig

Hang Glider

The Hang Glider's single wing rides on air. With just the right push, it smoothly swoops across the room.

MATERIALS

- 6-inch (15-cm) square of paper

START HERE

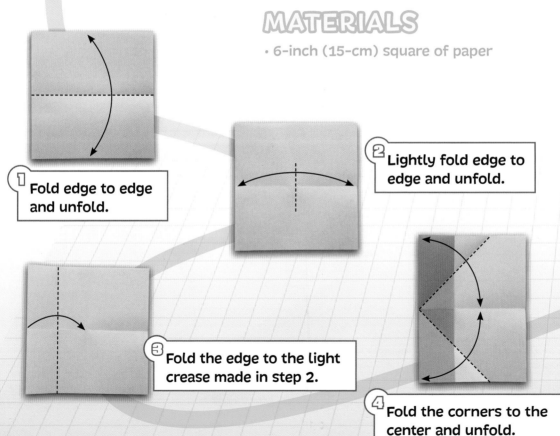

1. Fold edge to edge and unfold.

2. Lightly fold edge to edge and unfold.

3. Fold the edge to the light crease made in step 2.

4. Fold the corners to the center and unfold.

9 Finished
Hang Glider

END HERE

8 Fold the top
half behind
and unfold.

FLYING TIP

Pinch the back end of the wing.
Release with a gentle, forward push.
The higher you hold it at launch,
the farther it will glide.

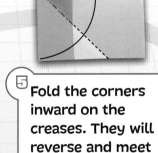

5 Fold the corners
inward on the
creases. They will
reverse and meet
in the center.

6 Fold the point.

7 Fold the flaps and tuck
them into the pockets
of the point.

Hoop Glider

Few paper airplanes sport the unique style of the Hoop Glider. This ring-shaped wing will surprise you with how well it sails.

START HERE

MATERIALS

- 6-inch (15-cm) square of paper

1 Fold point to point.

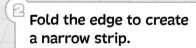

2 Fold the edge to create a narrow strip.

3 Fold again.

4 Bend the model to bring the ends of the strip together.

7 Finished Hoop Glider

END HERE

5 Tuck one end of the strip inside the other as far as it will go.

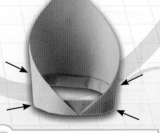

6 Shape the ring into a smooth circle.

FLYING TIP

Hold the pointed end of the plane. Release the Hoop Glider with a gentle, forward push. Hold it high when you launch it to make it glide farther.

Flapped Flyer

The Flapped Flyer is the perfect plane for testing flight patterns. Simply adjust the elevator flaps on the wings to change how the plane soars.

START HERE

MATERIALS

- 8.5- by 11-inch (22- by 28-cm) paper
- scissors

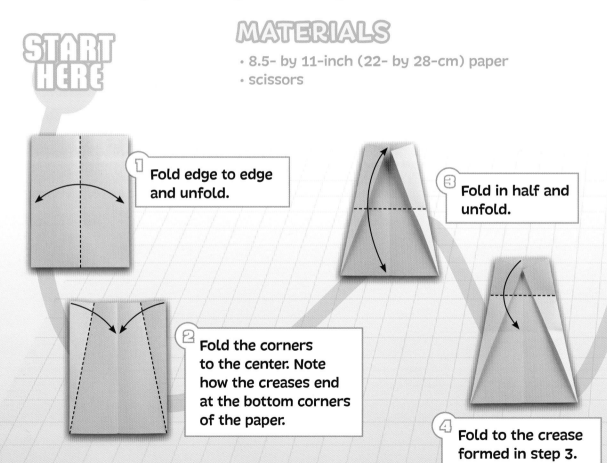

1 Fold edge to edge and unfold.

2 Fold the corners to the center. Note how the creases end at the bottom corners of the paper.

3 Fold in half and unfold.

4 Fold to the crease formed in step 3.

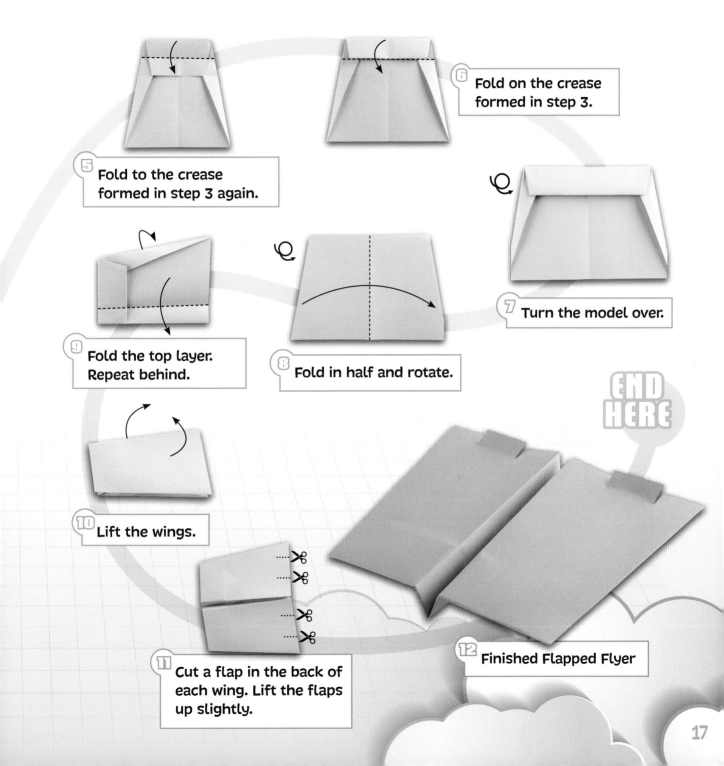

6 Fold on the crease formed in step 3.

5 Fold to the crease formed in step 3 again.

7 Turn the model over.

9 Fold the top layer. Repeat behind.

8 Fold in half and rotate.

END HERE

10 Lift the wings.

11 Cut a flap in the back of each wing. Lift the flaps up slightly.

12 Finished Flapped Flyer

Duck Plane

Don't let the Duck Plane's strange look fool you. This flat-nosed aircraft can handle crash landings and keep flying.

START HERE

MATERIALS

- 8.5- by 11-inch (22- by 28-cm) paper

1 **Fold edge to edge and unfold.**

2 **Fold the corners to the center.**

3 **Turn the paper over.**

4 **Fold the edges to the center. Allow the flaps behind to release to the top.**

18

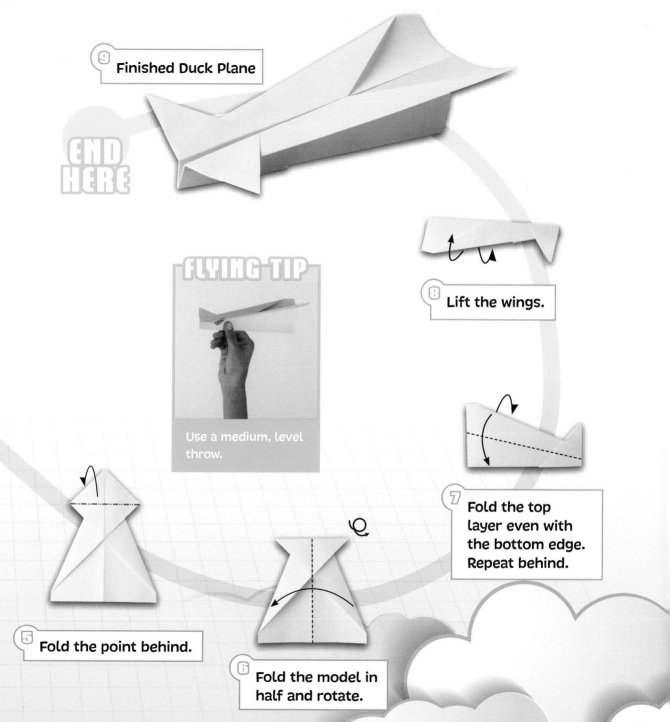

Finished Duck Plane

END
HERE

FLYING TIP

Use a medium, level throw.

⑧ **Lift the wings.**

⑦ **Fold the top layer even with the bottom edge. Repeat behind.**

⑤ **Fold the point behind.**

⑥ **Fold the model in half and rotate.**

Arrow

The Arrow may be the best long-distance flier you ever fold. With the right throw, it flies straight up to 45 feet (14 meters).

START HERE

MATERIALS

• 8.5- by 11-inch
  (22- by 28-cm) paper

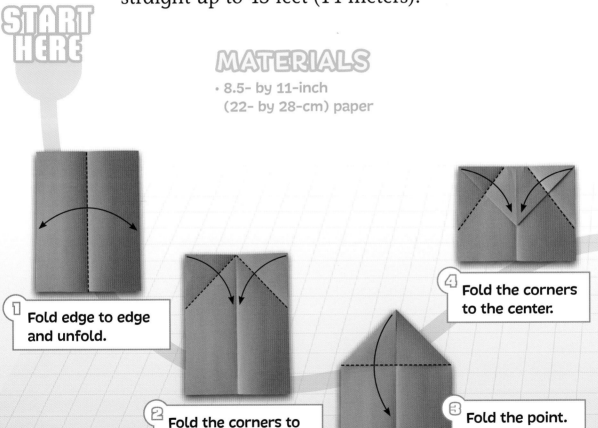

1. Fold edge to edge and unfold.

2. Fold the corners to the center.

3. Fold the point.

4. Fold the corners to the center.

20

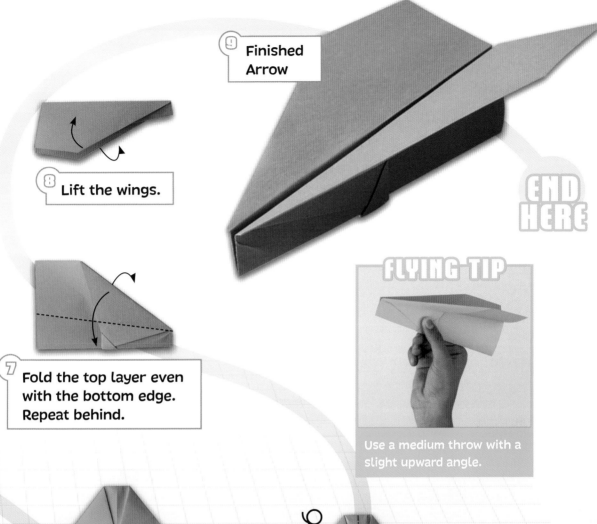

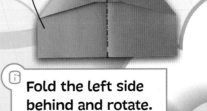

9 **Finished Arrow**

END HERE

8 **Lift the wings.**

7 **Fold the top layer even with the bottom edge. Repeat behind.**

FLYING TIP

Use a medium throw with a slight upward angle.

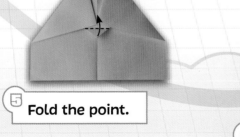

5 **Fold the point.**

6 **Fold the left side behind and rotate.**

Nosedive

Most planes are made for smooth landings. But the Nosedive prefers a big crash. Throw hard, and this plane twists and turns all the way to the ground.

MATERIALS

• 8.5- by 11-inch (22- by 28-cm) paper

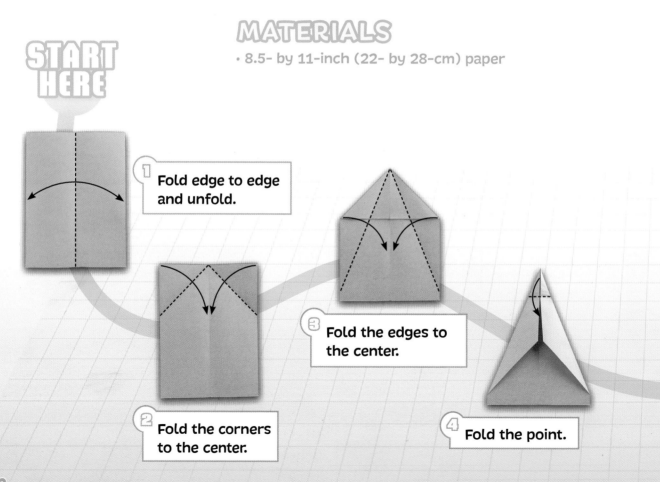

START HERE

1 **Fold edge to edge and unfold.**

2 **Fold the corners to the center.**

3 **Fold the edges to the center.**

4 **Fold the point.**

9 Finished Nosedive

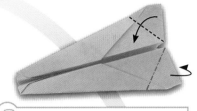

8 Fold one corner up slightly. Fold the other corner down slightly.

FLYING TIP

Use a strong throw with a slight upward angle.

7 Lift the wings.

5 Fold the model in half and rotate.

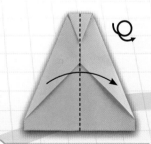

6 Fold the top layer even with the bottom edge. Repeat behind.

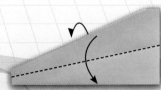

Read More

Harbo, Christopher L. *Easy Origami Toys*. Mankato, Minn.: Capstone Press, 2011.

Jackson, Paul. *Origami Airplanes*. Layton, Utah: Gibbs Smith, 2012.

Rau, Dana Meachen. *Making a Paper Airplane and Other Paper Toys*. Ann Arbor, Mich.: Cherry Lake Publishing, 2013.

Internet Sites

FactHound offers a safe, fun way to find Internet sites related to this book. All of the sites on FactHound have been researched by our staff.

Here's all you do:

Visit *www.facthound.com*

Type in this code: 9781491420478

Check out projects, games and lots more at
www.capstonekids.com